Hey, Peanuts!

Selected Cartoons from
MORE PEANUTS VOL. 2

Charles M. Schulz

CORONET BOOKS
Hodder Fawcett, London

Coronet edition 1970
Ninth impression 1978

Printed in Great Britain for Hodder
Fawcett Ltd., Mill Road, Dunton Green,
Sevenoaks, Kent. (Editorial Office:
47 Bedford Square, London, WC1 3DP) by
C. Nicholls & Company Ltd
The Philips Park Press, Manchester

ISBN 0 340 10761 8

AH? AH? AH?

AHCHOO!

THAT WAS AWFUL!

THAT WAS THE WORST PIANO PLAYING I'VE EVER HEARD!!

YOU HAVE ABSOLUTELY NO TALENT WHATSOEVER!

I'M HELPING SCHROEDER TO GET USED TO CRITICISM...

SCHULZ

© 1970 United Feature Syndicate, Inc.

Wherever Paperbacks Are Sold

FOR THE LOVE OF PEANUTS

All these books are available at your local bookshop or newsagent or can be ordered direct from the publisher. Just tick the titles you want and fill in the form below.

Prices and availability subject to change without notice.

〜〜〜〜〜〜〜〜〜〜〜〜〜〜〜〜〜〜〜〜〜〜〜〜〜〜〜

CORONET BOOKS, P.O. Box 11, Falmouth, Cornwall.
Please send cheque or postal order, and allow the following for postage and packing:
U.K. – One book 22p plus 10p per copy for each additional book ordered, up to a maximum of 82p.
B.F.P.O. and EIRE – 22p for the first book plus 10p per copy for the next 6 books, thereafter 4p per book.
OTHER OVERSEAS CUSTOMERS – 30p for the first book and 10p per copy for each additional book.

Name...

Address...

....